# Sparrows

# A Comedy

Charles Mander

*Samuel French—London*
*New York — Sydney — Toronto — Hollywood*

Copyright © 1980 by Charles Mander
All Rights Reserved

*SPARROWS* is fully protected under the copyright laws of the British Commonwealth, including Canada, the United States of America, and all other countries of the Copyright Union. All rights, including professional and amateur stage productions, recitation, lecturing, public reading, motion picture, radio broadcasting, television and the rights of translation into foreign languages are strictly reserved.

ISBN 978-0-573-12258-3

www.samuelfrench.co.uk
www.samuelfrench.com

## FOR AMATEUR PRODUCTION ENQUIRIES

### UNITED KINGDOM AND WORLD EXCLUDING NORTH AMERICA

plays@SamuelFrench-London.co.uk

020 7255 4302/01

Each title is subject to availability from Samuel French, depending upon country of performance.

CAUTION: Professional and amateur producers are hereby warned that *SPARROWS* is subject to a licensing fee. Publication of this play does not imply availability for performance. Both amateurs and professionals considering a production are strongly advised to apply to the appropriate agent before starting rehearsals, advertising, or booking a theatre. A licensing fee must be paid whether the title is presented for charity or gain and whether or not admission is charged.

The professional rights in this play are controlled by Samuel French Ltd, 52 Fitzroy Street, London, W1T 5JR.

No one shall make any changes in this title for the purpose of production. No part of this book may be reproduced, stored in a retrieval system, or transmitted in any form, by any means, now known or yet to be invented, including mechanical, electronic, photocopying, recording, videotaping, or otherwise, without the prior written permission of the publisher. No one shall upload this title, or part of this title, to any social media websites.

The right of Charles Mander to be identified as author of this work has been asserted in accordance with Section 77 of the Copyright, Designs and Patents Act 1988.

# CHARACTERS

Joyce
Harold Makepiece
Edward
Sandra

The action takes place on the esplanade of a small West Country resort

Time—the present

# AUTHOR'S NOTE

*Sparrows* was originally intended to run in conjunction with *The River* and *Monmouth* (both of which are also published by Samuel French Ltd). The characters in all three plays are interchangeable in roughly the same age group and the plays could be performed together under the title *The River*, although they are, of course, three separate plays, but linked by the river and the theme of pollution versus nature and employment versus the environment.

# SPARROWS

*A corporation shelter on the esplanade of a small West Country town. Just before lunch on an autumn day*

*The shelter is the type that contains a bench in the front facing the sea, and a bench at the back facing a slightly depressed backdrop of boarding-houses and a fish-and-chip shop. The shelter has a partition with a broken window that divides the two benches. It has been fairly substantially vandalized and written upon. We are concerned with that part of the shelter which faces the sea, which is the audience. It is set more or less C, and if possible on a small rostrum. L of it and further downstage there stands a post with a little roofed house that contains a lifebelt. Not far away on the same side of the stage is one of those curious wooden boxes containing deckchairs and painted with the words B.U.D.C. R of the shelter and also downstage, there stands a telescope on a pedestal which, providing you put sufficient money into its guts, provides a limited view of part of the Welsh coast R and an interesting view of a nuclear power station situated in the middle distance. The unseen power station is the modus vivendi of the play. The rest of the setting can be garnered with a NO PARKING sign, a flagpole with a limp red flag and anything else that catches the producer's fancy*

*As the play begins, two figures are discovered, one in the shelter and one fiddling with the telescope. The figure in the shelter is that of an ageing lady whose name is Joyce. She is surrounded by plastic shopping bags and is wearing numerous woollen but rather shabby garments covered with a torn plastic macintosh. The weather is uncertain for this is autumn and the holiday-makers who do not exactly flock to this drab seaside town, have long since departed— except for one. Harold Makepiece is an impecunious, redundant Civil Servant in his late fifties, he is respectably dressed in serge trousers, a linen jacket and a straw hat. He is occupied at the moment with the telescope, which does not function*

**Joyce** (*emerging from the shelter and scattering the crumbs from a Bath bun on to the ground*) Chuck-chuck—chuck-chuck . . .

(*She looks hopefully up in the air*) Come on chuckies—din-dins.
(*She stands hopefully for a moment waiting for her visitors. But
they do not come. She frowns sadly, shakes her head and turns
her attention to Harold*) It doesn't work.

**Harold** (*looking up and smiling nervously*) Oh.

**Joyce** It hasn't functioned for several years.

**Harold** Hasn't it?

**Joyce** No. (*She looks up into the air*) I daresay it's the seagulls.

**Harold** Pardon?

**Joyce** (*staring across the water at the invisible power station*) But
I doubt it. (*She frowns severely. Back to Harold*) Seagulls are
voracious creatures, you see—greedy—somewhat lacking in
principles. You must be a tourist.

**Harold** Pardon?

**Joyce** Otherwise you would have known.

**Harold** Known what?

**Joyce** About the telescope. You'd have saved your money.

**Harold** Yes—I would—er . . .

**Joyce** And now it's gone—down the drain. Have you seen any
sparrows?

**Harold** What?

**Joyce** (*looking upwards again*) I can't think what's happened.
(*Glaring out to sea*) But I suspect.

**Harold** Do you?

**Joyce** Yes. Ah well, we shall see—yes, by jove, we shall see. (*To
Harold*) That contraption gave up the ghost several years ago.
(*She goes back to her birds*) Chuck-chuck. Chuck-chuck.

**Harold** I think they should have put up a notice.

**Joyce** (*gazing at Harold*) How very odd . . .

**Harold** Oh no—I wouldn't have thought that it was odd at all—
common courtesy . . .

**Joyce** (*going back into the shelter*) You'd better come inside.
There's a free seat. (*She pats the bench beside her*)

**Harold** I'm quite all right, thank you.

**Joyce** You'd be better off out of the rain.

**Harold** It doesn't look like rain—hardly a cloud.

**Joyce** That's nothing to go by. There's a storm brewing. You
take my word for it.

**Harold** Well—I . . . All right then. If you say so. (*He joins her on
the bench*)

**Joyce** Splendid. One can't be too sure you know—this time of the year. You are a little late for the season if I may say so Mr—er?

**Harold** Makepiece—Harold Makepiece.

**Joyce** You're a little late for the season, Mr Makepiece, they've all gone. (*She looks out sadly*) Like the sparrows. (*After a moment*) Do you like sparrows, Mr Makepiece? Are you—er—simpatico?

**Harold** I haven't really thought about them—er—much.

**Joyce** Sad—sad—so many people just put sparrows out of their minds, Mr—er—Makepiece—take them for granted. But they are God's creatures you know, the same as ourselves.

**Harold** I suppose they are.

**Joyce** Some people don't like sparrows. (*Raising her voice a little*) Some people that I know personally don't like sparrows at all. (*She speaks to the window*) They become positively abusive when it comes to sparrows. Gosh, Mr Makepiece, I'm so glad I found you.

**Harold** (*embarrassed*) Do you—I mean—do you live here?

**Joyce** (*her face crumpling a little*) Yes.

**Harold** It must be nice.

**Joyce** (*quietly*) Do you think so?

**Harold** Oh yes—charming place.

**Joyce** Yes.

**Harold** I mean—well, there's the sea.

**Joyce** The sea.

**Harold** Well—yes, the sea. (*He peers out towards the audience*) More or less. And the climate's bracing. Wouldn't you say?

**Joyce** If the seagulls don't swoop down, the dogs eat up the crumbs. It's very hard on the sparrows.

**Harold** I expect they can look after themselves.

**Joyce** Can they? Do you really think so?

**Harold** There's plenty about. Never any shortage of sparrows. Must be millions.

**Joyce** I don't think that's relevant—Mr—er—Makepiece. One only has to think of the Indians.

**Harold** I'd rather not.

**Joyce** Ah. (*She looks at him shrewdly*) You must be a city dweller.

**Harold** I'm afraid so. But it's not a matter of choice. Circumstances do not allow—er . . .

**Joyce** I find sparrows companionable. I have quite a little circle of sparrows you know. There's Herbert and Violet and Francis and Bill and their children—little scamps, and Neddy and Gordon and Mrs Watkins—quite a circle.

**Harold** Remarkable.

**Joyce** What makes you say that?

**Harold** Well—sparrows to my way of thinking are sparrows.

**Joyce** I don't care for seagulls as a rule, I find them far too brash. But then one mustn't generalize, and I have to admit that I have been acquainted with the odd seagull who has been perfectly charming.

**Harold** (*nonplussed*) Oh . . .

*They sit in silence for a moment or two*

Do you come here often?

**Joyce** Every day, except when the weather is inclement. (*Her face crumples into sadness*) Then I stay at home—with Gilbert.

**Harold** Your husband?

**Joyce** Oh no—Gilbert's a canary.

**Harold** A what?

**Joyce** A canary.

**Harold** Yes—I should have guessed.

**Joyce** Gilbert's very nice in his way, but he lacks enterprise. He will cling to his perch, he seems happy to sit about in his cage all day and twitter. So I leave him to it—and come here and talk to my sparrows.

**Harold** Ah. (*He gets up*) Well—er—I ought to be popping along, you know. Time and tide waits for no man . . .

**Joyce** (*anxiously*) Don't go Mr Makepiece. You mustn't go. You are so suitable.

**Harold** (*hesitating*) Well—you see . . .

**Joyce** If you go you'll get caught in the rain, and you haven't got a raincoat.

**Harold** But . . .

**Joyce** And I shall be left alone with nobody to talk to—except Edward and he's most unreliable with sparrows.

**Harold** All right. But I can't stay for long, I have affairs, you understand, to attend to. I'm—a fairly busy man, you know

**Joyce** I expect you're an executive.

**Harold** (*pleased*) Well—in a manner of speaking.

**Joyce** Splendid—splendid. Couldn't be better. Quite a number of my sparrows are executives, Herbert's an executive. Always busy, always darting about here and there, he worries a lot, you can tell that. His feathers keep falling out.

**Harold** (*humouring her*) And what about Edward?

**Joyce** Who?

**Harold** Edward, you said he was unreliable with sparrows. Is he a magpie?

**Joyce** Good heavens no! Edward is *Homo sapiens*.

**Harold** Human?

**Joyce** More or less.

**Harold** Ah. Well, it makes a change.

**Joyce** (*diving into one of her bags*) Would you like a Bath bun?

**Harold** Pardon?

**Joyce** A Bath bun. It's really for the sparrows, but they haven't turned up and if I throw it on the ground the dogs will eat it.

**Harold** Er—no, thank you.

**Joyce** It's quite all right—I bought it in the Co-op.

**Harold** No—really—thank you. I've—er—just eaten.

**Joyce** What a pity. Never mind, I daresay Edward will scoff it, he never says no. Only it's such a business with him, one has to do it surreptitiously.

**Harold** Why? Why?

**Joyce** Because Sandra gets offended, and then there's a set-to.

**Harold** (*utterly mystified and therefore changing the conversation*) That building—(*he points across the water*)—over there. It's very imposing.

**Joyce** (*getting up and peering in the direction he is pointing*) What building?

**Harold** The big one—it really is enormous and curious looking...

**Joyce** It might be the new Town Hall. The old one met with an accident.

**Harold** I hardly think so, it looks more like some kind of power station.

**Joyce** (*indifferently*) Oh, that one. We don't talk about it, we pretend it isn't there.

**Harold** Why?

**Joyce** We think it's killing the sparrows. Anyway Edward and Sandra are going to blow it up. I wish you'd change your mind about the Bath bun, I do hate set-to's.

**Harold** It makes you proud—a building like that—it makes you proud to be British. Who did you say was going to blow it up?
**Joyce** Edward and Sandra. (*She holds up the Bath bun*) Just have a little nibble, it's quite tasty.
**Harold** No thank you. I really should toddle along ...

*A scruffy, hairy apparition appears, head and shoulders behind the glass partition that separates the back and front of the shelter. He is a man and that is about all you can tell. This is Edward, and he is making faces*

(*Seeing him and jumping back alarmed*) Oh my God!
**Joyce** Pardon?

*Edward reaches out through the broken glass, siezes the bun from Joyce's hand and disappears. As Joyce speaks, Harold starts to make off*

(*With a little squeak of surprise*) Ah! Bless my soul. Such a naughty boy. (*She jumps on to the bench and speaks through the window where Edward has disappeared*) You are a naughty boy, Edward. You know how Sandra feels about Bath buns. Well you'd better finish it now you've started. And do be quick. I want you to meet Mr Makepiece, I think he's the very person. (*She darts after Harold and takes him gently but firmly by the arm*) Don't go Mr Makepiece, Edward is longing to meet you, he'll be round in a moment. (*She guides Harold to the bench*) Yes—you are the very person. (*She looks at him admiringly. Then she jumps on to the bench and looks through the window once more*) Hurry up Edward, Mr Makepiece is ... Oh drat! (*She cranes her head through the window*) Edward? Edward? Where are you?
**Edward** (*sidling round the edge of the shelter*) Here.
**Joyce** (*giving another little squeak*) Ah! Silly boy.

*Edward has the appearance of a middle-aged teenage drop-out. He is extremely hairy, bedecked with beads and displays one elaborate ear-ring. He wears faded and unsavoury jeans, an embroidered and equally unsavoury waistcoat and flip-flop sandals. He is munching the remains of the Bath bun and dropping the crumbs down his beard. Harold edges away from the apparition in some alarm*

**Joyce** (*to Harold*) Don't be alarmed Mr Makepiece, Edward is quite harmless. Just unreliable. Now then come along Edward and say how-do-you-do to Mr Makepiece.

**Edward** How-do-you-do—brother. (*He sidles up to Joyce*)

**Harold** Er—good day.

*Edward whispers urgently into Joyce's ear*

**Joyce** No—no—of course not. (*She giggles*) Silly boy. (*To Harold*) He thinks you're from the Welfare.

*Harold smiles weakly*

Of course he's not from the Welfare, Edward. Mr Makepiece is an executive. Now what do you think of that?

**Edward** (*considering for a moment, his jaws masticating the final bits of Bath bun*) Not much.

**Joyce** Edward's a revolutionary, Mr Makepiece.

**Harold** Oh. (*He edges even further away*)

**Edward** (*obligingly*) Castrate the bosses! Up the workers!

**Joyce** (*sharply*) That's enough Edward! You'd better dispose of those crumbs on your whiskers, before Sandra returns. She's our leader Mr Makepiece—such a nice person, but a little forceful.

**Harold** I think perhaps I ought to . . . (*He starts to get up*)

*Joyce pushes him back firmly*

**Edward** (*brushing his beard with his fingers: anxiously*) Don't tell her Joyce—for Pete's sake don't tell her.

**Joyce** (*severely*) I'm not a sneak Edward. Sandra doesn't approve of carbohydrates, Mr Makepiece. She allows Edward only natural foods, seaweed and mussels and things. She's out foraging on the sea shore this very moment.

**Harold** Really?

**Joyce** Yes. But you see Edward has a weakness for Bath buns . . .

**Edward** I could do with another . . . (*He reaches for a paper bag*)

**Joyce** Certainly not! They're for the sparrows. (*She smacks his hand away*)

**Edward** (*morosely*) There aren't any sparrows.

**Joyce** That's neither here nor there. Besides, they'll be back. Why do you think I've invited Mr Makepiece to our little conference?

**Harold** Conference? Oh, I see. There's to be a conference.

Where? (*He brightens considerably, but not for long*)
**Joyce** Here.
**Harold** Where?
**Joyce** Right here, Mr Makepiece.
**Harold** But I thought ...
**Joyce** We're not a very large movement you see, in fact our entire membership can fit into this shelter. But small is beautiful, Mr Makepiece, and we are handy for the sparrows.
**Edward** Goddam sparrows!
**Joyce** (*warningly*) Edward!
**Edward** Taking the Bath buns out of the mouths of the workers.
**Joyce** They have to eat too, you know.
**Edward** Give 'em worms, then.
**Joyce** Worms are not easily available.
**Edward** Neither are Bath buns, for workers. (*He belches*) Who are starving.
**Joyce** Nobody, Edward, in the widest sense of imagination, could describe you as a worker.
**Edward** I go down the social security!
**Harold** Excuse me—may I ask ...?
**Joyce** That has nothing to do with it. Workers presumably—work.
**Edward** Sparrows don't.
**Harold** I am wondering if ...
**Joyce** Yes they do! They're always working—dashing here and there pecking at things. How can you be so perverse, Edward? Sometimes you can be most upsetting.
**Harold** (*raising his voice*) You mentioned a conference. (*Lowering it again*) You did mention a conference.
**Joyce** (*glaring at Edward*) Yes—I did—until somebody interrupted.
**Edward** Ah! Knickers! (*He plonks himself down and starts to scratch*)
**Harold** Perhaps you could enlighten me. You see I am not absolutely certain in my own mind what this conference, that you mentioned, is about.
**Joyce** But I thought I told you, Mr Makepiece.
**Harold** I cannot recollect an agenda, I must admit.
**Joyce** We don't issue agendas, Mr Makepiece. That would be far too dangerous. There are spies everywhere.

**Harold** Spies?
**Edward** And fascists.
**Harold** Good heavens!
**Joyce** So there is no agenda, and we can't start until Sandra gets back and we have a quorum.
**Harold** Oh—I see. (*Making another attempt at getting clear*) I really ought to toddle along—I do have . . .
**Joyce** She won't be long, Mr Makepiece, I promise you, and when she comes we can all get down to it.
**Harold** But am I necessary? Am I really necessary?
**Joyce** You are manna from heaven, Mr Makepiece. Of course you're necessary. (*Sharply*) Edward, stop scratching and tell Mr Makepiece that he is necessary.
**Edward** Eh?
**Joyce** You heard me.
**Edward** Well—I don't reckon he is.
**Joyce** Don't be perverse.
**Edward** I was going to do it. Everybody said that I was going to do it.
**Harold** Do what?
**Edward** Blow it up.
**Harold** (*alarmed*) Blow what up?
**Edward** That. (*He points across to the power station*)
**Harold** I don't understand. You don't mean . . .?
**Joyce** I did tell you, Mr Makepiece.
**Harold** But I thought you were joking . . .
**Joyce** At this moment, Mr Makepiece, sparrows and seagulls and starlings and great tits and little tits and woodpeckers and—
**Edward** Workers . . .
**Joyce** (*glaring at Edward*) Don't interrupt! Woodpeckers, Mr Makepiece, and so many of our feathered friends are being done to death by that monstrous thing over there. It is destroying nature, Mr Makepiece, it is polluting the air. Think of the birds and the bees, Mr Makepiece, think of them and you will know that I was not joking.
**Harold** (*with alarm*) Yes, but you see, I mean—I don't see what I have to do with it? I'm—I'm on holiday.
**Edward** What did I tell you? He's no bloody good, he's on holiday.
**Harold** You're absolutely right.

**Edward** She's bonkers. Got a sparrow fixation.

**Joyce** (*furiously*) How dare you, Edward. How can you? After all those Bath buns.

**Edward** Bloody sparrows! Shitting all over the pavements.

**Joyce** I'll never feed you again, Edward, not another Bath bun. You'll have to make do with seaweed.

**Harold** (*hopefully*) Good gracious, look at the time. I must be off.

*Harold starts to wriggle free, but Joyce, in spite of her agitation, clings on to him*

*Sandra comes in from the foreshore*

**Joyce** Oh Sandra—thank goodness you've come. We've found a man.

*Sandra is a small fiery woman in a long crumpled dress, gumboots, and similar beads to Edward. She is carrying a large canvas shoulder-bag laden with seaweed and various crustacea*

**Sandra** (*accusingly*) You've been feeding him.

**Joyce** Oh no.

**Sandra** Yes you have, you've been stuffing him with buns. It's all down his beard.

**Joyce** Oh—Edward? I thought you were referring to Mr Makepiece. (*She titters*)

**Sandra** Who?

**Joyce** This is Mr Makepiece. (*With pride*) I found him.

**Sandra** Where?

**Joyce** He was looking through the telescope.

**Sandra** He's not from the Welfare?

**Joyce** No—he's an executive. I thought he might do.

**Sandra** Were you followed?

**Harold** Er—no.

**Sandra** (*to Edward*) You greedy bastard! You're heading for scurvy—did you know that?

**Edward** Where's scurvy, Sandra?

**Sandra** (*plonking down the bag*) What do you think I've been doing all morning? Clambering about in mud and oil slicks.

**Edward** (*resignedly*) Collecting seaweed.

**Sandra** Exactly, so that you can grow big and strong and healthy and be a credit to the movement, and not a torpid pig stuffed with Bath buns. (*She takes a dead sparrow from her pocket*)

I found this on the foreshore. (*She hands it to Joyce*) Please accept my deepest sympathy.

**Joyce** (*lamenting in little wails*) Oh! Oh! It's Herbert! Poor—poor Herbert! This is truly awful! (*She holds him to her bosom tenderly*)

**Edward** (*muttering*) Bloody sparrows ...

**Sandra** (*fiercely*) Shut up!

**Edward** Well, if that had been a worker ...

**Sandra** (*to Joyce*) Why don't you go and bury him, dear—along with the others.

**Joyce** Yes. Poor Herbert. He was an executive, Mr Makepiece, like your good self.

**Harold** I am most awfully sorry—great tragedy.

**Joyce** (*bursting out*) It's that beastly thing! That beastly edifice! Blow it up, Mr Makepiece, blow it up before they all die. Oh—Herbert—Herbert—cut off in your prime. I shan't be a jiffy.

*Joyce hurries off with Herbert clutched to her breast*

*Harold tries to steal off*

**Sandra** (*crisply*) Sit down, Mr Makepiece.

**Harold** I was ...

*Edward moves round to block Harold's exit, and leers at him*

**Sandra** You were leaving.

**Harold** I—er—intrusion—grief—not seemly ... (*He comes face to face with Edward*) Oh.

**Sandra** Sit down—please.

**Harold** Oh—thank you. (*He sits*)

**Sandra** (*looking at him appreciatively*) I think we've found the very person. Executive type, mature, well-balanced, with a touch of the Civil Servant. The very person.

**Edward** One of *them*, if you ask me!

**Sandra** I didn't. (*To Harold*) Joyce told you I expect, she usually does. It's one of her weaknesses, indiscretion. I've had to speak to her about it on several occasions, but it makes no difference.

**Edward** That old sparrow-freak. She'll have us all inside again, Goddam nut! (*He sidles towards the Bath buns*)

**Sandra** (*smacking him away from them*) Oh no you don't! Keep your grubby hands off the carbohydrates.

**Edward** I was only going to sit down, Sandra.
**Sandra** Balls! Hop it! (*She waves him away*) Go and help Joyce
with the funeral.
**Edward** But I don't like sparrows, Sandra.
**Sandra** Then you'll enjoy burying one.
**Edward** Effing sparrows!

*Sandra glowers at him*

All right, I'm going. I know when I'm not wanted. (*Defiantly,
as he goes*) But I'm not singing any bloody hymns, and that's
final!

*Edward stamps out in a rage*

**Sandra** (*after Edward has gone*) I suppose you think we're mad,
Mr Makepiece.
**Harold** (*trying to sound convincing*) Oh no. Not at all.
**Sandra** I wouldn't blame you if you did—and you wouldn't be
the first. One only has to think of the Jews and Pharisees in the
context of Jesus of Nazareth. Goodness knows what they must
have thought of that motley collection of peasants. But they
changed the world, Mr Makepiece. (*She looks out to sea in a
dreamy fashion*) Yes, they changed the world—and for the
better I daresay. Which is our task.
**Harold** Is it? Er, is it really? Well I never . . . (*His voice trails off
helplessly*)
**Sandra** It's the world that's mad, Mr Makepiece, not us. We are
just the casualties of that madness, the victims. But since the
three of us have banded together we have been reborn. We
have discovered ourselves because we have a cause.
**Harold** Ah, yes—a cause.
**Sandra** Take Edward for instance. He was a lost soul, utterly
confused, wandering aimlessly through life stuffed with
carbohydrates and reeking of alcohol. I found him the other
side of this shelter in a semi-paralytic doze embracing two litre
bottles of farmhouse cider and a bag of potato crisps. The
bottles were, of course, empty.
**Harold** Ah . . .
**Sandra** But I revived him, fed him up on seaweed, dried him out
and gave him a cause and he lives again. And it's the same with
Joyce. The Joyces of this world have always been victims, Mr

Makepiece. Always. (*She pauses for a moment and stares out to sea*)

**Harold** (*quietly*) I too am redundant—getting on a bit you see. But I'm not convinced that your cause is—er . . .

**Sandra** Have you been to the water's edge, Mr Makepiece? Have you paddled?

**Harold** No. It never seems to be within reach somehow, I must confess.

**Sandra** Everything is in reach—if you strive. (*She looks at him and he turns away*) Even that monstrosity over there.

**Harold** I hope it isn't—I really hope it isn't—I'm sorry but . . .

**Sandra** If you go down to the water, Mr Makepiece, you will notice its colour. And you will see what is in it. Because this is an estuary and the river that feeds it is polluted. The beach is polluted. And the madmen who are responsible for it have built a temple and there it stands. One amongst thousands springing up like rodent ulcers, poisoning the atmosphere, destroying nature, disfiguring mankind. It must be torn down, we must rend the temple, Mr Makepiece, tear it from the face of the earth. Before it is too late.

**Harold** But in that case, how are we going to run our central heating?

**Sandra** Central heating, Mr Makepiece? Are you also prepared to worship at that temple? To preside over the inevitable devastation of our countryside, the murder of our people, in order to run your central heating?

**Harold** Well, put that way, I suppose . . .

**Sandra** Of course not, Mr Makepiece, you are a sensible man, a sane man. You are going to help us blow it up.

**Harold** Oh no! No. It's not my line of country. I have no experience in that sort of thing. I was in Agriculture and Fisheries.

**Sandra** You don't need experience. All you have to do is plant the device.

**Harold** The what?

**Sandra** The device. It's quite simple, it's in a box, it's not heavy.

**Harold** You're—you're—joking—a box did you say?

**Sandra** Yes.

**Harold** (*leaping up and peering about*) Oh dear me. Oh dear, dear me. Is that the time? I shall be late for lunch.

*He tries to make off, but Sandra prevents him by jumping in front of him*

**Sandra** You can have lunch with us. (*She indicates the seaweed*)
**Harold** NO! I mean—well—it's most kind of you. Oh yes. (*He looks round despairingly*) I—er—I have a peptic ulcer—have to be very careful—might burst any moment. Excuse me ... Oh my God—what's that?

*Edward and Joyce can be heard singing "All Things Bright and Beautiful", off*

**Sandra** They are mourning the departed. The dead. Today a common sparrow—tomorrow ...?
**Harold** Couldn't you go through the proper channels? I am sure that if you approached your local Council ...
**Sandra** All tried, Mr Makepiece, and found wanting. Beaurocrats, Mr Makepiece, incompetent, arrogant, indifferent. Not interested in mankind, only themselves and their paper empires. I despise them.
**Harold** Nevertheless ...
**Sandra** There is no substitute for direct action. You must know that. Bombs, Mr Makepiece—explosives—that's all they'll listen to.
**Harold** This is insane. (*He wrings his hands*) Utter madness. I can't believe that in this ... (*His expression changes*) You're pulling my leg. You are pulling my leg. (*He laughs*) You're playing a prank on me. Oh dear—(*he laughs again*)—what an old silly I am. Oh dear me, you did catch me with my trousers down.
**Sandra** Would you like to see the device?
**Harold** Of course—of course—anything you like. (*He laughs again*) Does it tick?
**Sandra** (*going to Joyce's bag and producing an evil black box*) Yes, Mr Makepiece, it does tick. (*She hands it to him*)
**Harold** So it does. (*He shakes it*) How remarkable.
**Sandra** I wouldn't shake it if I were you. Explosive devices in this category tend to be a little unreliable.
**Harold** Well, well. How extraordinary. Can I have a peep inside?
**Sandra** I wouldn't advise it. It's booby-trapped. I built a rather

cunning little make-and-break circuit that trips the firing mechanism when the box is opened.

**Harold** Fascinating—absolutely fascinating. I daresay you're an expert.

**Sandra** Oh yes. I have a Ph.D. I wrote my thesis on explosives, Mr Makepiece. And I worked for three years in an ordnance factory on explosive gases. That's what opened my eyes.

*Harold goes white*

Don't drop it, Mr Makepiece. It's quite safe as it stands, but one shouldn't take unnecessary risks.

**Harold** No—no—of course not . . . Ah . . .

**Sandra** Perhaps I had better have it back. (*She takes the bomb from Harold's palsied hands*)

**Harold** I—I . . .

**Sandra** What?

**Harold** I—I—thought you were joking—but you're not—you're not—are you?

**Sandra** No, Mr Makepiece. I'm sorry . . .

*Harold slides down dazedly on to the bench*

*Joyce and Edward enter*

**Joyce** That makes twenty-six. It really can't go on like this, it's approaching genocide and I'm running out of little crosses. We sang "All Things Bright and Beautiful". So appropriate. Edward has a splendid voice, and he knew the words, he must have been a choirboy. What's the matter with Mr Makepiece, Sandra? He looks quite done in.

**Sandra** I have been showing him the device.

**Joyce** Isn't it splendid, Mr Makepiece. Sandra's so clever. The last one she made blew up the Town Hall.

**Harold** Oh no . . . (*He buries his head in his hands*)

**Joyce** It was quite all right, it was after office hours, there was nobody there, and they put it down to the I.R.A.

**Edward** Bloody disgrace! Those bastards get all the credit.

**Joyce** I do hope that Mr Makepiece has made up his mind to help us.

**Sandra** I think he has.

**Harold** (*wildly*) No! No!

**Sandra** (*swinging the case about casually*) There's nothing to it. All you have to do is plant this device.

**Harold** Please be careful . . .
**Joyce** It's quite safe, Mr Makepiece, I carry it about all the time.
Just in case . . .
**Harold** In case of what?
**Joyce** Eventualities. One never knows when somebody like you
will turn up.
**Harold** I wish I hadn't.
**Joyce** Think of the sparrows, Mr Makepiece. Gird your loins.
**Harold** I'm not well. I'm going to have a heart attack—call an
ambulance.
**Edward** (*producing a small bottle from his pocket*) Here drink this.
**Harold** What is it?
**Edward** Methylated spirits.
**Harold** NO!
**Sandra** Are you with us, Mr Makepiece, can we count on you?
**Harold** I can't give you an immediate decision. I was in the Civil
Service. Oh dear—this is all so bizarre—unbelievable. I'd be
happier if you put that bomb away, madam, before we all get
transported to glory.

*Edward starts to drink the methylated spirits*

**Sandra** (*crossly*) Oh, very well, if it frightens you. (*She gives the
bomb to Joyce*) Put it with the Bath buns, it might discourage
Billy Bunter . . . (*She sees Edward swigging at the bottle*) Lay
off that muck! Do you want to ruin your guts! (*She swipes it
from his lips*)
**Edward** (*spitting and choking*) Jesus Christ! You nearly had my
teeth out. And my guts are ruined anyway. How can a man live
on seaweed?
**Sandra** (*disdainfully*) You're not a man. You're a walking dustbin.
**Edward** Watch it, Sandra. Revolutionaries can get nasty.
**Sandra** Shut up!
**Edward** What?
**Sandra** Shut up!
**Edward** O.K.
**Harold** You're making a big mistake.
**Sandra** (*to Edward*) What did you say?
**Edward** Eh?
**Joyce** It was Mr Makepiece, Sandra. He was making a
pronouncement.

**Harold** I think you're making a big mistake. You can't blow up a nuclear power station.

**Sandra** Why not?

**Harold** It isn't feasible.

**Sandra** It's perfectly feasible. We've done our homework, we're not fools. We're not aiming for the reactor, you know. We don't want Armageddon, Mr Makepiece. All we require is a little bang in the control room—to make a point.

**Harold** But you'd never get in. I mean, there's no point in blowing something up if you can't get into it. I think we should all go home.

**Sandra** We're not getting in, Mr Makepiece, you're getting in.

**Harold** Me? But look here—I'm just a bystander. You can't involve me in your diabolical plans. I . . .

**Sandra** Now calm down—and look at it sensibly. Our plans are not diabolical. We are striving for the salvation of mankind.

**Joyce** And sparrows.

**Edward** And the workers—don't forget them.

**Harold** With respect—with great respect—I cannot see what purpose you are serving on behalf of mankind or sparrows by blowing up a power station. And I am afraid I shall have to decline your offer—and go home.

**Sandra** But you haven't heard our plan yet.

**Harold** I'm not sure that I want to. The only thing I'm sure about is that something has gone wrong—terribly wrong. It may be me. But it has gone wrong. Because one moment I was simply walking—strolling—taking a constitutional along this splendid esplanade, minding my own business and then suddenly I am hurled into what can only be described as a nightmare. A bizarre, unbelievable nightmare, in which people—no— lunatics surround me with bombs and expiring sparrows and suggest—no—demand that I personally blow up a nuclear power station. It's not on, you know. It's just not on.

**Edward** Is he talking about us? I'm not a lunatic—I'm a worker.

**Joyce** Poor man. He's going off his head.

**Sandra** I'm going to boil up some seaweed for lunch, Mr Makepiece, it's very nourishing. You'll feel better for it.

**Harold** (*writhing*) NO! Spare me that . . .

**Sandra** Then when the tide comes in, Edward can paddle you across in the coracle.

**Harold** Coracle? What coracle? What are you talking about?
**Sandra** Our coracle. Edward made it out of reeds and mud, it's quite safe.
**Joyce** He carries it on his head.
**Harold** (*beating himself*) Wake up! Wake up!
**Sandra** He'll deposit you on the power station jetty, and all you have to do is walk in and plant the device. It couldn't be easier.
**Harold** (*writhing*) Let me go! You're insane! Insane!
**Sandra** (*with dignity*) It's the world that's insane, Mr Makepiece. Not us.
**Joyce** They're destroying the birds of the air, Mr Makepiece, with their infernal machines. The little sparrows—how can anyone in their right mind do that?
**Edward** I could. Bloody pests!
**Joyce** Don't say things like that Edward—not even in jest.
**Sandra** Sparrows, workers, giraffes, what's the difference? They're all God's creatures, and they're doomed.
**Harold** Where are the police in this town? For God's sake where are the police? You can never find them when you want them . . .
**Joyce** You can't expect them to be everywhere—it's lunchtime.

*Harold groans and beats his forehead*

**Sandra** We know it's not easy for you, Mr Makepiece. We understand that. But you are vital to our plans, you can make history.
**Harold** Why? Why? Why pick on me?
**Sandra** Because you're the only person here who could gain entry to that place.
**Harold** How do you know? How do you know?
**Joyce** You're an executive, Mr Makepiece. You can get in anywhere.
**Sandra** And you're wearing a collar and tie.
**Joyce** Don't think we haven't tried on our own account, Mr Makepiece. Edward rowed across last Wednesday but the coracle sprung a leak. He had to swim for it.
**Edward** I could have drowned.
**Joyce** And Edward isn't suitable. You see, he's known to the authorities.
**Harold** Well, that doesn't surprise me . . .

**Sandra** This is our last safe house. If they find this it's curtains.

**Joyce** (*again proudly*) Edward has done time.

**Edward** That's right. That's how I found out about the workers—and Bath buns.

**Sandra** You see, you see how they work, these madmen. They destroy the people with carbohydrates and destroy the environment with effluence. Even the seaweed is polluted. We appeal to you, Mr Makepiece, in the name of sanity, we appeal to you.

**Harold** I'd much rather go home.

**Sandra** You are lucky to have a home, Mr Makepiece. Edward and I don't. We live on the beach and in this shelter and Joyce has a damp basement and a canary. Everything else has gone to the movement.

**Joyce** We're not complaining. One has to make sacrifices. One has to think of the sparrows.

**Edward** And the workers.

**Sandra** All our possessions went into the device, bombs are not cheap you know. And we don't like robbing banks, that's dishonest.

**Harold** No—I'm very sorry—but absolutely and definitely no. I can't agree with you. There is no excuse for violence. None whatever. Blowing things up is no answer to any problem. You should pursue your aims through the proper channels. Supposing everybody went about with bombs, blowing things up. Have you thought of that? Have you thought of the chaos? Just imagine the confusion you must have caused in the Town Hall, all those files and forms in triplicate, destroyed at a stroke. It doesn't bear thinking about. And as for the power station . . . No. No. I can't help you. I'm sorry—I'm not very good in boats, I get seasick.

**Sandra** Is that your last word?

**Harold** Yes, I'm afraid it is. I would not draw the line at a determined attempt through the proper channels, or even, *in extremis*, a small peaceful demonstration. Because I think you have a point. But expecting me to hazard my life upon the ocean in a leaking coracle in order to blow up a nuclear power station. Well that's really not on. And neither, all things considered, is it very practical.

**Sandra** (*going to the Bath bun bag and returning with the bomb*) What are we going to do with this then?

**Harold** Well I don't know.
**Sandra** I've primed it.
**Harold** You've what?
**Sandra** It's due to go off at two o'clock.
**Harold** Well stop it! Stop it!
**Sandra** I can't. It's set and that's that.
**Harold** Well, throw it into the sea! I don't want it.
**Joyce** Don't panic, Mr Makepiece. (*She consults her "watch"*)
It's barely one forty-five.
**Edward** You haven't got a watch.
**Joyce** Yes I have. (*She consults her wrist*) Oh—you're right I
haven't. How very observant you are Edward.
**Edward** I nicked it.
**Joyce** Oh, you naughty boy.
**Harold** Good God! Does nobody know the time?

*Edward surreptitiously helps himself to a Bath bun*

**Sandra** (*crisply*) We'll have to do it ourselves. Edward!
**Edward** What?
**Sandra** Put that filthy thing down and get the boat. (*She puts the
case to her ear*) It's stopped ticking.
**Harold** OH MY GOD! (*He crouches into a protective ball*)
**Sandra** Well don't stand about ruminating Edward, there's not a
moment to lose. You'll have to paddle like hell. Come along
Joyce. (*She starts to go*)

*Edward goes*

**Joyce** (*hovering beside Harold*) So nice to have met you, Mr
Makepiece. (*She gathers up her belongings in a leisurely fashion*)
I'm sorry that you couldn't see your way to assisting us in our
great adventure.
**Harold** Yes. Good-bye. Good-bye. (*He waves her away*)
**Joyce** I know that you have a fellow feeling for the sparrows . . .
**Harold** (*desperately*) Yes, yes—splendid creatures. Good-bye.
**Joyce** Poor Herbert's under the sod now. How many more, Mr
Makepiece? How many more?
**Harold** Spare me—spare me! I'm not ready!
**Joyce** Poor Herbert was definitely an executive person, like
yourself. He always went through the proper channels, that
was his downfall. Because you see, by the time he had finished

doing everything in the correct manner, there was nothing left for him to do. And no crumbs, because he'd been so busy going through the correct channels, that the others had gobbled up the Bath buns. Poor Herbert—no wonder his feathers drooped.

**Sandra** (*coming back with the bomb*) Hurry up, Joyce, for goodness sake. This thing is beginning to hiss.

**Harold** (*getting under the bench*) Dear God! Not now! Not now! I'm only here on holiday.

**Joyce** Good-bye, Mr Makepiece. Good-bye, sparrows. I'm ready now, Sandra. Isn't it exciting—let's sing a little hymn. Edward has such a lovely voice, I'm sure he must have been a choir-boy.

*Joyce trails out with Sandra*

*Harold crouches under the bench, his hands over his ears. Edward and the others can be heard singing "All Things Bright and Beautiful" in the distance. After a few phrases the singing is drowned by a large and devastating explosion. The Lights dim for a moment, things drop on to the stage. Harold crouches terrified under the bench. After a moment Joyce can be heard calling*

**Joyce** (*off*) Mr Makepiece? Mr Makepiece?

*Harold emerges trembling and looks heavenward*

**Harold** Who's that? Who's there?

*Joyce trots in*

**Joyce** Well, what do you think of that?

**Harold** (*looking at her with his mouth open*) Great God! (*He looks at her in horror*) Is it you?

**Joyce** Well of course it's me.

**Harold** It's a miracle—a miracle—how are the otheis?

**Joyce** Oh they're all right, they're on the beach. Sandra's cooking seaweed. She says it's the last supper. The beginning and the end. Sometimes she gets quite lyrical—and rather inaccurate. It's too early for supper.

**Harold** But the bomb? The bomb? It went off. It exploded like the dickens. I was nearly eliminated.

**Joyce** It wasn't our bomb, Mr Makepiece. Isn't it wonderful how the Lord works? We didn't need our bomb. In fact, Sandra threw it away after that place went up.

**Harold** What place? For God's sake, woman—what are you talking about?

**Joyce** The power station, Mr Makepiece. Isn't it wonderful, we didn't need our bomb after all. It blew itself up. The power station blew itself up. God works in mysterious ways, Mr Makepiece. Sandra says come and join the last supper.

*Joyce takes Harold gently by the arm. The Lights slowly fade as though a shadow is coming over the face of the earth. Edward and the others are heard singing "All Things Bright and Beautiful", as—*

the CURTAIN *falls*

# FURNITURE AND PROPERTY LIST

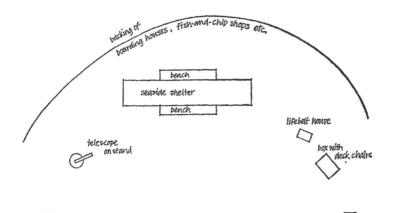

*On stage:* Esplanade shelter. *On front bench:* plastic shopping bags
containing Bath buns, black box bomb, dressing
Small roofed house with lifebelt
Wooden box with deck chairs
Telescope on pedestal
"NO PARKING" sign, flagpole (optional)

*Personal:* **Harold:** watch
**Sandra:** large canvas shoulder-bag full of seaweed and
crustacea, dead sparrow
**Edward:** small bottle of methylated spirits

# LIGHTING PLOT

Property fittings required: nil
Exterior: A seaside esplanade

*To open:* General effect of autumn midday light
*Cue* 1    After explosion    (Page 21)
          *Lights dim, then return to normal*
*Cue* 2    Joyce takes Harold's arm    (Page 22)
          *Slow fade to* CURTAIN


# EFFECTS PLOT

*Cue* 1    As hymn is sung    (Page 21)
          *Loud explosion*

MADE AND PRINTED IN GREAT BRITAIN BY
LATIMER TREND & COMPANY LTD PLYMOUTH
MADE IN ENGLAND

Lightning Source UK Ltd.
Milton Keynes UK
UKOW06f2209070416

271787UK00003B/7/P